Michelle Obama

CHRISTINE TAYLOR-BUTLER

Children's Press®
An Imprint of Scholastic Inc.
New York Toronto London Auckland Sydney
Mexico City New Delhi Hong Kong
Danbury, Connecticut

Content Consultant
James Marten, PhD
Professor and Chair, History Department
Marquette University
Milwaukee, Wisconsin

Library of Congress Cataloging-in-Publication Data
Taylor-Butler, Christine.
  Michelle Obama / by Christine Taylor-Butler.
     pages cm. — (A true book)
  Includes bibliographical references and index.
  Audience: Grades 4–6.
  ISBN 978-0-531-21192-2 (library binding : alk. paper) — ISBN 978-0-531-21206-6 (pbk. : alk. paper)
  1. Obama, Michelle, 1964—Juvenile literature. 2. Presidents' spouses—United States—
Biography—Juvenile literature. 3. Legislators' spouses—United States—Biography—Juvenile lit-
erature. 4. African American women lawyers—Illinois—Chicago—Biography—Juvenile literature.
5. Chicago (Ill.)—Biography—Juvenile literature. I. Title.
  E909.O24T59 2015
  973.932092—dc23 [B]   2014031010

All rights reserved. Published in 2015 by Children's Press, an imprint of Scholastic Inc. Published
simultaneously in Canada. Printed in China 62.
SCHOLASTIC, CHILDREN'S PRESS, A TRUE BOOK™ and associated logos are trademarks and/or
registered trademarks of Scholastic Inc.
1 2 3 4 5 6 7 8 9 10 R 24 23 22 21 20 19 18 17 16 15

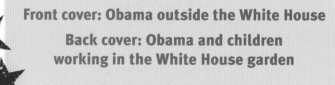

Front cover: Obama outside the White House

**Back cover: Obama and children
working in the White House garden**

Find the Truth!

Everything you are about to read is true *except* for one of the sentences on this page.

Which one is **TRUE**?

T or F Michelle Obama followed her brother to Harvard University.

T or F Barack Obama was Michelle's intern at a Chicago law firm.

Find the answers in this book.

Contents

THE BIG TRUTH!

From Martha to Michelle

The first family

Michelle exercises for 90 minutes every day.

Michelle as a young girl

CHAPTER 1

Bright and Determined

Michelle LaVaughn Robinson was born on January 17, 1964. Her family lived in a modest neighborhood on the south side of Chicago. Her father, Fraser, worked for the Chicago Water Department. Her mother, Marian, stayed home to raise Michelle and her older brother, Craig. Neither parent attended college, but both had high hopes for their children.

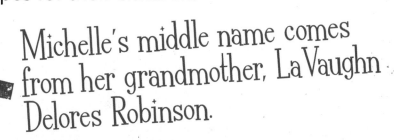

Michelle's middle name comes from her grandmother, LaVaughn Delores Robinson.

A Loving Family

Michelle's family rented a small one-bedroom apartment in her great-aunt's **bungalow**. Spending time together was very important to the family. They ate meals together, read books, and played board games such as Monopoly and chess. The house was filled with laughter. Marian and Fraser encouraged Michelle to pursue her interests.

Michelle and her brother were allowed to watch only one hour of television each day.

Michelle's childhood home in Chicago

Michelle attended Bryn Mawr Elementary School, pictured here.

Fast Learner

Michelle was a very bright and independent child. She taught herself to read before she started kindergarten. When she started elementary school, her parents gave her an alarm clock. Michelle used the clock to get herself out of bed in time for school every morning. She did so well in school that she was allowed to skip second grade. She went right from first grade to third grade.

National Honor Society

Michelle (second from right) poses with fellow members of the National Honor Society.

Michelle often spent her free time practicing the piano.

School Days

Michelle worked hard in her classes. In sixth grade, she started attending special classes for gifted students. She remained in this program through eighth grade. This helped her gain admission to Whitney M. Young Magnet High School, which only accepted the most talented students.

Star Student

Michelle earned a place on the honor roll each year during high school. She was also **inducted** into the National Honor Society. In addition to her studies, she sang in the school choir and was elected to the student council. In 1981, Michelle was named **salutatorian** of her graduating class. This means she had the second-best grades of all the students in her class.

Michelle (left) and her fellow student council members pose for a yearbook photo.

Never Say Never

When it was time to choose a college, Michelle immediately thought of Princeton University. Her older brother, Craig, was already a student there. Michelle wanted to join him. However, her high school counselors told her that her test scores weren't quite good enough to get into such an elite college.

Princeton University, in New Jersey, is considered one of the top universities in the nation.

Michelle and her brother, Craig, have a very close relationship.

Off to College

Michelle's parents had taught her to always question what she had been told. She wanted to make her parents proud. Instead of listening to the counselors at her high school, she applied to Princeton anyway. Her plan paid off when she received a letter saying that she had been accepted. She joined Craig on campus in the fall of 1981.

Michelle poses for a yearbook photo at Princeton.

CHAPTER 2

From Ivy League to Public Service

Out of the 1,141 freshmen in Michelle's class, there were just 94 black students. Life at Princeton was difficult for African American students. They were often treated poorly by their white classmates. Michelle's first roommate was moved to another dorm after the girl's mother filed a complaint with the university. She didn't want her daughter sharing a room with an African American.

 Princeton was founded in 1746.

Making Her Own Way

Even though African American students were often treated like outsiders, Michelle soon found ways to pursue her interests at Princeton. She once said, "Every time somebody told me, 'No, you can't do that,' I pushed past their doubts and I took my seat at the table."

Michelle worked at Princeton's Third World Center, which provided a variety of resources to the university's minority students.

Michelle's mother, Marian (pictured here), taught her to always speak her mind.

Early Riser

Classes at Princeton were difficult, but Michelle was determined to succeed. Each morning, she woke up early to study. She and a friend were often the first ones in the dining hall for breakfast. Michelle also spoke her mind about problems she noticed at the school. She even told teachers that they weren't teaching French classes correctly. Michelle's mother once told a reporter, "If it's not right, she's going to say so."

Big Brother Craig

Michelle's brother, Craig, was a big part of her community at Princeton. Craig was a popular student and a star player on the school's basketball team. He went on to become the fourth-highest scorer in Princeton's history. When Michelle became a vocal activist on campus, Craig complained to their mother that it was hurting his reputation at school. Marian told him, "Just pretend you don't know her!"

Remembering Her Roots

Michelle majored in sociology, the study of human social behavior. She wrote a research paper on how racial identity changes in college. She contacted 400 black **alumni** who had attended Princeton in the 1970s. Nearly 100 of them wrote back. Many said that their time at Princeton had caused them to lose touch with their African American roots. Michelle was determined to prove she could succeed at college without losing her ties to the black community.

Michelle minored in African American studies.

Michelle poses for her graduation photo at Princeton.

Law School

In 1985, Michelle graduated **cum laude** from Princeton. With such an important honor from a respected school, she had many options when it came time to decide her next move. Michelle knew she wanted to help people. She decided that the best way to do this was to become a lawyer. She traveled to Cambridge, Massachusetts, to attend Harvard Law School.

Harvard is one of the top law schools in the country.

Aside from Michelle, the only other first lady with a law degree is Hillary Clinton.

Barack Obama began attending Harvard Law School the same year Michelle graduated.

Michelle during her time at Harvard

Helping Out

Michelle worked hard at Harvard. In addition to her regular classes, she continued her study of the effects of college on black students. In her free time, she worked with the Harvard Legal Aid Bureau. The bureau provided free legal services to people who couldn't afford to hire lawyers. In 1988, Michelle received her law degree. It was time for her to join the working world as a lawyer.

Michelle and Barack Obama
spent Christmas together in
Hawaii in 1989.

CHAPTER 3

Meeting Barack

After graduating from Harvard, Michelle went to work for Sidley Austin, a law firm in Chicago. There, she had many important assignments. However, she did not feel challenged, so she asked for harder work. Instead, in 1989, she was given an **intern** to supervise. He was a tall, scrappy young student from Harvard Law School. When she saw his name, she thought, "Who names their kid Barack Obama?"

A law degree is called a Juris Doctor.

In 1991, Barack helped register 150,000 new voters in the Chicago area.

Young Barack plays on the beach with his grandfather, Stanley Dunham.

Not Quite Love at First Sight

When Michelle first met Barack, she was not very impressed with him. But she began to like him more after hearing about his interesting life story. He had grown up in Hawaii, but he had also lived in Indonesia. And before going to Harvard Law School, Barack had worked as a community organizer in Chicago. There, he had worked in neighborhoods near Michelle's childhood home.

Turning Down a Date

After a few weeks of work at the law firm, Barack asked Michelle to go on a date with him. Though she liked Barack, she turned him down. As his supervisor at work, she didn't think it would be right to go out with him. Barack wasn't ready to give up so easily, though.

Barack was one of the top students in his class at Harvard Law.

A Change of Heart

Barack invited Michelle to a community meeting in the basement of a local church. At the meeting, he told people about how they could work to change their lives. Michelle was very impressed with the way people responded to his words. She thought he was special. One month later, she finally agreed to go out with him as long as he didn't call it a date.

On their first date, Barack and Michelle went to a museum and a movie.

As a community organizer, Barack encouraged people to vote and play an active role in shaping their neighborhoods.

Craig and Barack have remained good friends since meeting for the first time.

Meeting the Family

Michelle soon introduced Barack to her family. Her father believed he could tell a lot about a person from the way that person played sports. Michelle asked Craig to play basketball with Barack. Barack was a good player, but he also knew when he needed to pass the ball to his teammates. Craig was impressed with this teamwork. Barack had passed the family "test."

Michelle and Barack at their wedding in 1992

Getting Married

Michelle and Barack grew more and more serious.
In 1991, Barack graduated cum laude from Harvard
Law School. Soon after, he asked Michelle to
marry him. Unlike the first time he asked her on a
date, she said yes right away. Michelle and Barack
were married on October 3, 1992.

A New Job

About a year before the wedding, Michelle had decided she wanted to work more closely with the community. She left Sidley Austin and took a job at the Chicago mayor's office. The pay was lower, but the job would allow her to make a difference. Michelle worked for the Department of Planning and Development. She soon became known for her ability to quickly solve any problems that came her way.

Michelle was very involved with Chicago's city government during the early 1990s.

From Martha to Michelle

Though first ladies are not chosen in elections, they still play important roles in the country's leadership. At first, they mainly served as hostesses during dinners or other formal occasions at the White House. Over time, however, many first ladies took a more active role in leading the nation. Today, most first ladies use their fame and influence to advance causes that are important to them.

Martha Washington

In 1789, Martha Washington became the nation's first first lady when her husband, George Washington, was sworn into office as the first U.S. president. Martha accepted her role as a public figure. However, she secretly disliked the lack of privacy that came with the job. She told friends that she would rather be at home.

Lucy Webb Hayes

The wife of President Rutherford B. Hayes, Lucy Webb Hayes was the first first lady to hold a college degree. After her husband was elected, she traveled across the entire country by train, which earned her widespread popularity. She was also the first to host an Easter egg roll on the White House lawn, which has since become an annual tradition.

Eleanor Roosevelt

Eleanor Roosevelt greatly expanded the role of the first lady during the presidency of her husband, Franklin Roosevelt. She traveled throughout the country to give speeches, and often published articles and papers about issues that were important to her, such as equal rights for women and African Americans. She remained involved in politics even after Franklin's death in 1945. She served as a U.S. representative to the United Nations.

Hillary Clinton

As first lady, Hillary Clinton worked closely with her husband, President Bill Clinton, to develop new laws and policies. After Bill left office, Hillary began her own political career. She served two terms in the U.S. Senate and was chosen by President Barack Obama to serve as the secretary of state during his first term.

Michelle and Barack pose with their daughters, Malia (second from left) and Sasha, for a photo in the White House's Oval Office.

CHAPTER 4

Family Matters

In 1996, Barack made a big career change of his own when he ran for and won a seat in the Illinois Senate. Soon after this, Michelle took a new job as associate dean of student services at the University of Chicago. Her experience with the students led her to think about starting a family.

Michelle sometimes calls herself "Mom-in-Chief."

A Growing Family

In July 1998, Michelle and Barack's first daughter, Malia, was born. Their second child, a daughter named Sasha, was born three years later. The new parents had their hands full caring for the children, but Barack's job often kept him away from home. In 2004, he decided to take his political career even farther. Michelle supported him as he **campaigned** and won a seat in the U.S. Senate.

The next year, she made a career advancement of her own when she was named vice president for community and external affairs at the University of Chicago Hospitals.

Michelle and Barack take baby Malia for a walk in Chicago in 2000.

The Obamas celebrate Barack's 43rd birthday during his 2004 Senate campaign.

Keeping Busy

As a working mother, Michelle was very busy. Barack was always on the campaign trail or working in Washington, D.C. Michelle stayed in Chicago to raise the girls. She joked to a local newspaper that life would be easier if her husband got a normal job. But Barack wasn't finished with his political plans. After many long discussions with Michelle, he decided to run for president in 2008.

The Campaign Trail

Michelle quit her job to help with Barack's presidential campaign. She traveled across the country delivering speeches and giving television interviews. Though the campaign was stressful, she kept a positive attitude. In November 2008, Barack won the election. This made Michelle the first African American first lady.

Timeline of Michelle Obama

January 17, 1964

Michelle LaVaughn Robinson is born in Chicago, Illinois.

1981

Michelle begins college at Princeton University.

A Normal Life

Michelle wanted the family to continue leading a normal life after Barack became president. Malia and Sasha clean their rooms and make their own beds in the White House. They also take care of their dog, Bo. Michelle's mother, Marian, lives in the White House, too. She helps take care of the girls when Barack and Michelle are busy with their jobs.

1988
Michelle graduates from Harvard Law School.

October 3, 1992
Michelle and Barack Obama are married.

2009
Michelle becomes the first African American first lady in U.S. history.

Michelle dances during an event celebrating the two-year anniversary of her "Let's Move" program.

CHAPTER 5

Starting a "Movement"

When Michelle was a busy working mother in Chicago, the family ate a lot of fast-food meals. Michelle began replacing these unhealthy foods with fresh fruits and vegetables. She saw positive results in her family's health. After becoming first lady, she decided to use her position to help spread healthy habits to other people throughout the nation.

To work out, Michelle lifts weights, runs on a treadmill, and kickboxes.

On the Move

In 2010, Michelle created the "Let's Move" program. It aims to fight childhood **obesity** by giving parents and children the support they need to make healthy choices. Exercise, access to affordable healthy food, and learning to eat

right are key ingredients for success. Michelle exercises daily and tours the country to show that exercise can be fun.

Michelle exercises with a group of students in 2011.

40

One of Michelle's favorite foods is chicken meatball noodle soup.

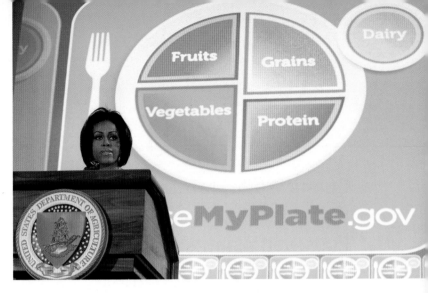

Michelle introduces the new MyPlate graphic to the public.

MyPlate

The U.S. government once used a graphic called the food pyramid to show people how much of each different kind of food they should eat. Many people thought it was confusing. In 2011, Michelle revealed an improved design. It was a plate and a glass showing the proper amounts of food a person should consume. This graphic, called MyPlate, was much easier for people to understand than the food pyramid.

Victory Gardens

During World War II (1939–1945), the United States faced a food shortage. First lady Eleanor Roosevelt planted the first White House vegetable garden in 1943. It was called a victory garden. Twenty million Americans were inspired to create gardens of their own. This helped to deal with the food shortage. By the end of the year, 42 percent of the country's vegetables were grown in home gardens.

Growing Fresh Foods

Michelle also created a vegetable garden on the White House lawn. Tomatoes, herbs, figs, rhubarb, broccoli, lettuce, and snap peas all grow there. A beehive even provides honey for tea. Thanks in part to Michelle's efforts, the nation is becoming a healthier place. ★

The National Park Service gives public tours of the White House garden for two days each spring.

Michelle harvests lettuce from the White House garden alongside a group of students.

True Statistics

Number of first ladies: 46

Earliest first lady to earn a college degree: Lucy Webb Hayes

Earliest first lady to earn a graduate degree: Pat Nixon

Earliest first lady to earn a law degree: Hillary Clinton

Earliest first lady to fly in an airplane: Eleanor Roosevelt on April 20, 1933

First White House library: Created by first lady Abigail Fillmore in 1850

Tallest first ladies: Eleanor Roosevelt and Michelle Obama, at 5 feet, 11 inches

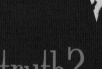

Did you find the truth?

F Michelle Obama followed her brother to Harvard University.

T Barack Obama was Michelle's intern at a Chicago law firm.

Resources

Books

Brill, Marlene Targ. *Michelle Obama: From Chicago's South Side to the White House*. Minneapolis: Lerner Publications, 2010.

Brophy, David Bergen. *Michelle Obama: Meet the First Lady*. New York: Collins, 2009.

Edwards, Roberta, and Ken Call. *Michelle Obama: Mom-in-Chief*. New York: Grosset & Dunlap, 2009.

Kesselring, Susan. *Michelle Obama*. Mankato, MN: Child's World, 2010.

Visit this Scholastic Web site for more information on Michelle Obama:
★ www.factsfornow.scholastic.com
Enter the keywords **Michelle Obama**

Important Words

alumni (uh-LUM-nye) — graduates or former students of a school, college, or university

bungalow (BUHNG-guh-loh) — a small house, usually with only one floor

campaigned (kam-PAYND) — organized action in order to achieve a particular goal, as in an election campaign

cum laude (KOOM LAU-duh) — a Latin phrase meaning "with honor," used to indicate top graduates from a school, college, or university

inducted (in-DUK-tid) — admitted into a club or organization

intern (IN-turn) — someone who is learning a skill or job by working with an expert in that field

obesity (o-BEE-si-tee) — the condition of being extremely fat

salutatorian (suh-loo-tuh-TOR-ee-uhn) — the member of a graduating class with the second-highest grades in the class

Index

Page numbers in **bold** indicate illustrations.

About the Author

Christine Taylor-Butler is the author of more than 75 books for children, including True Books about American history and government, health and the human body, and science experiments. A graduate of the Massachusetts Institute of Technology (MIT), Christine holds degrees in civil engineering and art and design. She currently lives in Kansas City, Missouri.